get good®
at
SLIDES

get good® at SLIDES

How to create presentation slides that make your message stick

Lee Jackson

"I once had a boss who would walk out of a meeting if there were more than 11 powerpoint slides. It was actually nothing to do with quantity, but everything to do with quality. It was because very few people knew how to use slides properly. I've often looked at this problem and though that presenters ask too much of technology and not enough of themselves. Well help is at hand... Powerpoint Surgery is an invaluable resource by my friend Lee Jackson aimed at helping you get the best out of your presentations. I certainly learnt a few things from it myself and I highly recommend it to anyone who needs to communicate a message to an audience in a memorable way. Whether that means a small group of young people, a boardroom of executives, or a keynote in front of a large audience, this book will help you think (and present) differently."

Jeremy Waite Head of Social Strategy, Adobe EMEA

"Lee Jackson is the man who takes PowerPoint presentations from boring to brilliant. If you take his straightforward advice, your audiences will love you, and your messages will hit home. I can't recommend him highly enough. Whether you're pitching for business, delivering internal presentations or speaking to conferences, Lee's advice will make you more successful."

Alan Stevens FPSA, Past President Global Speakers Federation and co-author of 'The Exceptional Speaker'

*"Jackson has got a bl**dy nerve asking me to write a testimonial for his book. It's like asking Mary Whitehouse to endorse '50 Shades of Grey'. You see, I am a proudly militant Anti-PowerPoint Bigot. The only presentational surgery I have ever recommended is a slide-ectomy. The thing that sickens me most is that he doesn't just reveal the moron-proof secrets of creating compelling slides. Instead, I found myself shamefully seduced into a new way of slide-enhanced thinking. Somehow, he has turned the Indefensible into the Indispensable. I now intend to quietly share my post-Surgery thoughts with my clients and pretend they were all my idea. Let's see if Jackson has got the balls to sue me."*

Graham Davies, author of 'The Presentation Coach'

"Lee's PowerPoint Surgery will help cut out the Death by PowerPoint that is plaguing presentations and meetings around the world. His simple, powerful techniques will instantly improve your slides – so that your talk has more impact and your message shines through and STICKS! His no-nonsense style, clear and succinct advice illustrated with examples and case studies mean that this book will be one you will return to time and time again."

Emma Sutton, Queen of Diamonds, NakedPresenting.co.uk

"Cuts through the noise and waffle that so often accompanies presentation best practice books and gives the reader something to work with immediately. The net result of reading Lee's book will be better presentations – great news for presenter and audience alike".

Simon Morton, Author of 'The Presentation Lab'

"Brilliantly delivered, perfectly executed – a masterclass of creating sublime slides & presentations, but be warned, you may never be able to sit through a presentation again without thinking of Lee Jackson!"

Geoff Ramm, President 2013 Professional Speaking Association UK and Ireland

"Lee takes a clever and refreshing approach to presentation mastery"

Nancy Duarte, author of 'Slide:ology', 'Resonate' and principal of Duarte.com, creators of the visuals for Academy Award-winning film, 'An Inconvenient Truth'.

ISBN 978-1-916230-70-5 Paperback
ISBN 978-1-9162307-1-2 Ebook

This edition published 2019

First published 2013 under the title:
'Powerpoint Surgery – How to create presentation slides that make your message stick'

Published by Get Good Books

Design and typesetting by Ashdown Creative

Printed in the UK

Printed on recycled paper

Some slides/photos used may be edited slightly for anonymity purposes

Disclaimer

All information in this book is correct and safe to use as far as we were able to establish, but please be sensible and always take precautions when changing or adding software to your computer. We cannot be held responsible for problems with your computer and cannot answer direct questions of a technical nature, please consult your I.T. Department, local PC shop or techie friend for help. We really believe that the information here will transform your slides but we also cannot be held responsible if your talk goes badly and you don't get that promotion or new account you went for!

Acknowledgements

Thanks to Nancy Duarte and Garr Reynolds and many other great slide designers and speakers whose ideas have inspired me to seriously think this issue through from my perspective as a professional speaker.[1] Their help and occasional social media encouragements have been very generous. Thanks to BigStockPhoto.com for their special offer to you and their help with stock images. Thanks to my friends and colleagues in the PSA, especially Alan Stevens, Paul McGee, Geoff Ramm, Derek Arden and others who have encouraged me to write and speak about this. Thanks to the amazing team at PSA Yorkshire. Thanks to Richard, Sarah, Will, Nathan, Emma Sutton for the re-drawing of the stick man, Simon, Simon Morton and JD for their input too. A special thanks to Pippa White for her keen eye, sense of humour, efficiency and editing skills.

...and finally to everyone whose good and bad slides inspired me to write the book I've been harping on about for years.

SLIDES ARE NOTHING NEW,
USED IN HERE IN 1905.

1984

Robert Gaskins[2] in his original proposal for the development of PowerPoint in 1984 (originally a Mac product) said that it was designed to 'improve the clarity of complex material'.

He's right it can do that, but strangely it can also do exactly the opposite.

INTRODUCTION

THERE ARE THREE BIG THINGS IN LIFE THAT WE RARELY GET TRAINED FOR – RELATIONSHIPS, PARENTING AND POWERPOINT.

Maybe three of the most important things in our lives and no-one ever bothers to give us training. Everything in life and business revolves around relationships. Parenting is still the biggest influence on the future of our children (even the newspapers can't argue with that). When making presentations the future of our business or career may just well hang in the balance. Not sure about that? Ask Gerald Ratner. On a more positive note, ask David Cameron, who, when he took off his jacket and did his 'I'm down with the people' talk at the Conservative party conference became Prime Minister in many people's eyes. Just as Boris Johnson hanging 20 feet up from a zip wire during the London 2012 Olympics may help him become PM too! Scary but true. Talks and therefore often slides, have a big impact on our future, so let's do them well. As a famous little green alien with long ears once said "**Do**, or **do not**. There is no **try**."

If you've read any presentation skills books, you may have picked up that people either ignore, advise badly, or are ever-so-slightly grumpy about the use of slides. And rightly so – many of us have had several painful PowerPoint experiences. For some this pain has become the norm. It's part of life, like death and taxes. It doesn't have to be like that.

3 Types of Speakers

There are 3 types of speakers in the world. The first love slides, they embrace them and they use them effectively to enhance their talks. They understand what makes a good slide and apply those rules for maximum impact.

The second don't use slides at all. They ignore them because they don't need them or they don't want to use them, and that's great. There are some excellent speakers in that category and I occasionally agree with them and do that myself. Not all talks need slides – eulogies are a classic example! Dr. Martin Luther King Jnr. didn't suffer from the lack of slides, neither did JFK or Obama.

However, I'm much more concerned about the third type of public speaker, a speaker who says they don't use or like slides but they use them anyway! This gets them into all sorts of trouble. An experienced speaker once told me,

"I WORK VERY HARD ON MY TALKS LEE, BUT I JUST THROW SOME SLIDES TOGETHER".

I didn't know what to say. He just wasn't bothered. He doesn't throw his stories and message together as he's a great speaker so why would he throw his slides together? It's bizarre.

A phrase that strikes fear into my heart is when a speaker stands and says;

"I HAVEN'T HAD TIME TO PREPARE SO I'M JUST GOING TO READ FROM MY SLIDES".

This is usually followed by the speaker turning their back on the audience to commence their public reading exercise. You may laugh but I have genuinely seen this.

Even worse, I've heard this: "I'm very nervous, so I'm just going to read from my slides, [they gave out a small nervous laugh] these aren't even my slides, and I haven't had time to look at them!". We thought he was joking – he wasn't. That's an hour of my life I'll never get back. Similarly a friend of mine who works for a speakers' bureau recalls how on her MA course one student copied the whole of their research paper onto slides and just read it out to the class with their back turned. Shocking stuff.

There is a better way.

This cut-to-the-chase guide will be an enema for some, which I hope, will cleanse them from within of their problem with slides! Some people do appear to need some sort of medical help with this issue. If bad PowerPoint truly is a disease, let me perform a little surgery to get to the heart of the matter…

By the end of this short book you'll have the philosophy, research and more importantly the practical tools to make great visual slides to make your message stick.

> **"If your words or images are not on point, making them dance in colour won't make them relevant... Power corrupts, PowerPoint corrupts absolutely.[3]"**
>
> **EDWARD TUFTE**
> YALE EMERITUS PROFESSOR

DON'T PASS ON THE BLAME

THE ENGRAINED BUSINESS PHILOSOPHY OF 'SLIDES ARE THE PRESENTATION'[4] IS A MAJOR PROBLEM THAT NEEDS ADDRESSING.

My philosophy is simple – if our slides are bad, don't blame the software, or our audience, it's our fault. If our football team loses, we don't blame FIFA (except for the lack of goal-line technology – don't get me started), we blame the manager, we blame the team. If our train is late, we blame the train operator, not George Stephenson! When I coach my business clients on slides they often say to me that their boss forces them to use 'the company slides', so not using the 'standard corporate slide pack' is seen as being rude or disrespectful to their boss. PowerPoint has waaaay too much power in the corporate world. It's not on the board, it's not a shareholder, we need to treat it as what it is – a piece of computer code that we can use for good, or for evil.

The software that we use, whether it's Microsoft PowerPoint, Apple Keynote (my programme of choice), Prezi, Slideshark, Haiku Deck or the various other open source programs out there, the issue remains the same.

All of these programs aren't inherently bad, they are neutral, they are just tools for us to use.

SLIDES SHOULDN'T BE BANNED BUT THEY SHOULD BE TAKEN INTO A DARK ALLEY, ROUGHED UP A BIT AND GIVEN A SERIOUS TALKING TO!

1841

In 1841 the new president of the United States was William Henry Harrison aged 68. His inauguration speech was a joyous occasion where he read a verbatim script of 8000 words, mainly about Roman civilisation. It was a cold day and a few days later he caught a bug which blossomed into pneumonia – he died 32 days later. No-one is totally sure, but he may well have literally killed himself with a boring talk. I'm guessing his audience wasn't too happy either. Thankfully he didn't have slides.

THE NEXT GENERATION ISN'T IMPRESSED LIKE I AM

MY DAUGHTERS TOLD ME THE OTHER DAY THAT 90% OF THEIR SCHOOL LESSONS ARE NOW ON POWERPOINT OR SMART-BOARD. WHY IS THAT?

Because it's easy to recycle our talks that way. I still remember how exciting PowerPoint was when I graduated from using an overhead projector in my years as a youth worker. But no one is impressed with a flashing word on a screen that moves and sparkles anymore. People are there to learn new stuff from you, not to see how fast the processor is on your laptop. Shiny, spinning 'word-art' just doesn't cut it. We must go back to basics.

Teaching yourself to use slides well, can **enhance** rather than hinder the presentation that you're making...

Here's why...

3 reasons to use great slides...

1. This is a visual generation

1

THIS IS A VISUAL GENERATION

THE NEW GENERATION IN THE WORKPLACE IS USED TO SEEING INTERACTIVE ADS ON THEIR COMPUTERS AND SMARTPHONES.

Screens have been vying for their attention from birth. They've never used a phone with a cord attached; they have grown up with targeted online ads and smartphones. Their phones have always had the internet on them. When I was in Japan recently it was a culture shock to be immersed in all that colour and all those flashing adverts. I'm not sure my teenage daughters even noticed, they just thought it was normal. I went to see Coldplay last year (don't judge me!), and as we walked into the arena, the whole place was in neon and we were all given a wristband to wear. When they started their first song the UV lights came on, lit up the whole arena and then our wristbands started flashing to the beat of the music. They continued on and off throughout the gig and even until we got into our cars in the car park. It wasn't a concert it was a full-on visual experience, much like the London 2012 opening ceremony. That is the world we live in.

2

VISUAL STAGES ARE THE NORM

I WAS AT ONE OF THE UK'S BIGGEST CONFERENCES LAST YEAR WHERE THE TRIPLE JUMPER JONATHAN EDWARDS WAS SPEAKING.

He measured his steps out across the stage showing the length of his world record jump (over 18 metres). The stage was enormous, with three massive screens dominating the hall, but the organisers put a small lectern in the left hand corner and most of the speakers spoke from behind that, many totally ignoring the twenty five metre stage **and** the three massive screens behind them. It was very dull. If they'd only walked the stage and had a few striking slides – people would have listened more. They didn't, and, they didn't. Yawnsville. It was one of the most boring days of my life, a true busman's holiday. Even at smaller events, the screen often takes centre stage, so if you don't want to have the organisers' dull maroon (or bright yellow) template behind you for the whole presentation then create your own slides, or the default *will* kick in. I've even seen inappropriate screen savers kick in after 20 minutes! No-one was ever inspired or moved to action with the 'default', (more on that later). Slides create your backdrop, they are your own green screen and canvas where you can show your personality, or shock/wake up a visual audience. Your slides won't seal the deal but they will oil the wheels.

3. Slides make your content stickier...
Glue Stick
Glue Stick

3

SLIDES REALLY CAN MAKE YOUR CONTENT STICKIER

NEED SOME PROOF? WELL, BIZARRELY, RESEARCH ON SLIDE DESIGN ISN'T IN ABUNDANCE AND MUCH OF IT IS COLLEGE, NOT 'REAL-WORLD' BASED.

There is a good piece of academic research on multi-media that I've found which shines a light on an up-to-now grey area: Principles of Educational Multimedia User Interface Design by Lawrence J. Najjar from the Georgia Tech Research Institute. He says this in his conclusion: "The most strongly supported principles suggest that designers should (a) use closely related verbal and pictorial information together and (b) build in tasks that encourage learners to elaboratively process the information."

He goes on to say: "There is strong empirical support...for the use of supportive pictures with verbal information." In layman's terms, when you are speaking about something, show a big picture that illustrates your words and always be interactive with the audience. That certainly supports my twenty years' of experience, speaking to some very challenging audiences.

If you speak only, people may remember up to 10% of what you say 72 hours later, but if you speak **and** show a relevant image their recall can go up to 64% after 72 hours![5] Even if that isn't super-accurate in all situations, it's still a massive improvement in recall – a revolution even, and it's well worth acting upon.

After you speak you usually get feedback one way or another, sometimes on post-event forms/emails, via twitter or face to face there and then. My involvement in coaching slide design for others first began when people started saying to me after my talks – "I really liked your slides". When this first happened I was slightly offended – don't you mean "I loved your jokes, and life changing content?" I thought arrogantly, but then the bell rang… "DING!". Other speakers' slides have been so bad that they have noticed a difference, so contrary to what some speakers tell you, visuals ***are*** noticed and they *can* make a difference. But only if they are done in the right way. Slides really don't have to be the last sausage on the speaker's barbecue.

STICKY

In their excellent book 'Made To Stick' Chip and Dan Heath share their research on the 'stickiness' of ideas, they share six principles of 'stickiness'. They say ideas should be Simple, Unexpected, Concrete, Credible, Emotional, Stories, bear this in mind as we talk about your presentations and slides. After all – why do a presentation that no-one wants to remember?

We need to ditch the corporate camouflage and be remarkable.

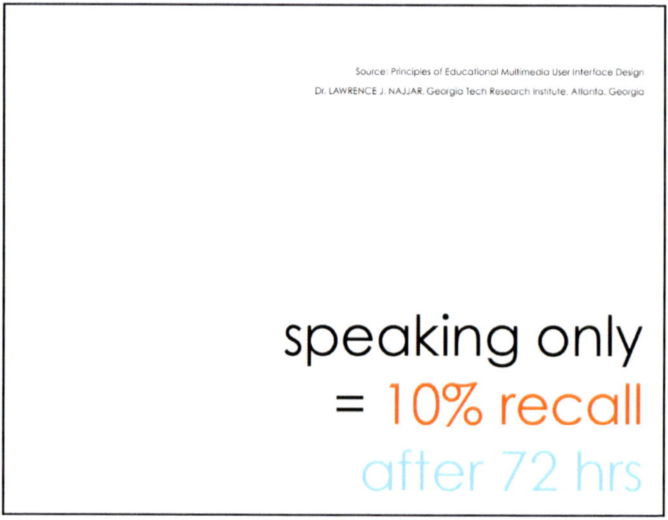
Source: Principles of Educational Multimedia User Interface Design
Dr. LAWRENCE J. NAJJAR, Georgia Tech Research Institute, Atlanta, Georgia
speaking only
= 10% recall
after 72 hrs

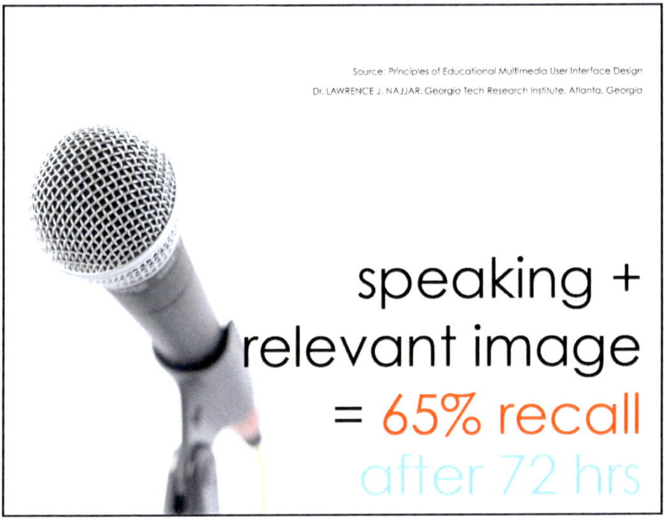
Source: Principles of Educational Multimedia User Interface Design
Dr. LAWRENCE J. NAJJAR, Georgia Tech Research Institute, Atlanta, Georgia
speaking +
relevant image
= 65% recall
after 72 hrs

POLICE

FIRSTLY, **STOP!**

BEFORE YOU OPEN YOUR SOFTWARE, STOP! HAVE YOU GOT TO THE 'NUB' OR 'CORE' OF YOUR MESSAGE? WHAT DO YOU WANT PEOPLE TO TAKE AWAY?

If you're not there yet, no number of slides will help you – in fact they'll make things worse. PowerPoint expert Simon Morton said to me "Presenters' biggest issue is that they start planning their talk with their software. Use a pencil and paper first". Always start to plan **away** from your computer. Once you're happy with the shape of your talk, then use blank cards or post-it notes to get the main points, and put them into the correct order. Then write very brief ideas for your slides i.e. "photo of donkey or photo of bridge" etc. Then and **only** then start up your presentation software. When I'm going to a new gig in the car I don't just start driving with the Sat Nav on random. I find out where I'm going, punch in the info and then set off. With my sense of direction programming a Sat Nav is a must – so is getting to the core of your message. My speaker friend Emma Sutton calls it 'finding your diamond'.

John Sweller developed Cognitive Load Theory,[6] often discussed in relation to slides used in presentations. The theory discusses the limited resources that our memory offers. In other words, for those of us delivering presentations, people's short-term 'working memory' is limited. So, they can listen to us *or* read a wordy slide but rarely do both at the same time. You are the presentation, ***not*** your slide text. That's why 'backdrop' or 'billboard' is the best way to think of slides. Don't overload peoples' often stressed out brains, they will simply switch off.

Cognitive load
theory

Think billboard not
document...

THINK BILLBOARD NOT DOCUMENT

THIS IS WHERE THE ROT SETS IN, PEOPLE SIMPLY TRY TO DO TOO MANY THINGS WITH THEIR SLIDES.

Fundamentally, slides are for the audience, not for us the speaker. Although I admit it's tempting, they should not be our crutch. Once we understand that they are for our audience, we design them in a bigger and bolder way. Feel free to make a word document to hand out after your talk if you like (although no-one ever reads those documents in my experience), but don't make your slides in that way. Build them for the bored bloke in row 33. Nancy Duarte helpfully compared slides to billboards in her book Slide:ology. Imagine you are passing your slides at 50mph on a major road. Could you read them as you drive past? If you can't they are too complicated and wordy. It's a simple but effective test for designers like us.

Design your slides and if appropriate write some handout notes.

BUT, JUST TO BE ABSOLUTELY CLEAR THEY ARE TWO VERY SEPARATE THINGS!

If you're going to produce a presentation slide deck, then do just that – don't be tempted to make it into a hand-out with a slightly larger font.*

The slide opposite is real, it's from a lawyers presentation. Informative handout, maybe, but a terrible slide! Many of the bad slides sent to me were from the legal profession. No comment.

**Garr Reynolds in his book Presentation Zen calls this a slideument!*

(logo removed)

What is a disqualification order and what is its purpose?

- *"The primary purpose of* [s.6 disqualification] *is not to punish the individual but to protect the public against the future conduct of companies by persons whose past records as directors of insolvent companies have shown them to be a danger to creditors and others"*

  (Browne-Wilkinson V.C. in *Re Lo-Line Electric Motors Ltd [1988] Ch. 477 at 486*)

- **Company Directors Disqualification Act 1986 ("the CDDA")**
- **s.1(1)** In the circumstances specified below in this Act a court may, and under sections 6 and 9A shall, make against a person a disqualification order, that is to say an order that for a period specified in the order -
  - (a) he shall not be a director of a company, act as receiver of a company's property or in any way, whether directly or indirectly, be concerned or take part in the promotion, formation or management of a company unless (in each case) he has the leave of the court, and
  - (b) he shall not act as an insolvency practitioner.

This is a document not a slide.

THE SLIDES ARE NOT YOUR SCRIPT

ONE OF PEOPLE'S MAIN OBJECTIONS TO CHANGING THE WAY THEY DO SLIDES IS THAT THEY USE THE SLIDES AS A SCRIPT, AUTO-CUE, OR AIDE DE MEMOIR (IF YOU'RE POSH!).

It doesn't have to be that way, there are many ways to stop using the bullet-point crutch.

Firstly top musicians don't use sheet music when they perform, they learn the piece but for the rest of us, here are a few tips:

Learn your talk (if it's something you're passionate about, you'll probably know it anyway). My fellow speaker David Hyner sometimes uses a tiny piece of card in the palm of his hand where he has little diagrams that keep him on track during a presentation, no-one knows it's there but he finds it useful at times. You can use small subtle cards with marker pen, not biro-sized notes on them, be careful where you place them and no-one will even notice (just don't tie them together with an old school treasury tag like someone doing a father of the bride speech and you'll be fine). For a longer presentation I personally print out my slides on 'hand-out view' five to a page portrait style and write Sharpie notes next to them then I place them in a display folder. I use them as a refresher before I go on stage and have them there as a backup, I may only glance at them twice in a hour, but for me I find that useful.

They are more to keep me on track rather than to tell me what to say. Find what works for you, be subtle and trust your abilities, no-one needs notes as much as they think they do.

Another speaker I know used to use loads of notes, then one day they fell off the table and went all over the stage. He just carried on speaking and he said that from that day onwards he realised he didn't need really them. He's never used notes since.

GREAT SPEAKING IS A PERFORMANCE NOT A RECITAL.

BLACK IS OFTEN BEST

For large audiences a black slide background often works best but for smaller audiences lighter is fine just be careful that the slides don't overpower you as the presenter. People want to see your face not just a silhouette.

YOU ARE A DESIGNER

WHETHER YOU LIKE IT OR NOT, AS SOON AS YOU OPEN YOUR SLIDE DESIGN PROGRAMME YOU INSTANTLY BECOME A DESIGNER.

My designer mate Paul Kerfoot had a go at me a while back when I said to him "I'm not a designer Paul, I just love making good slides". He made me realise that of course, we are all designers – it's not a choice we have once we use presentation software. The penny dropped.

Designer's Tip: Most designers, photographers and cameramen use 'the rule of thirds' aka the 'golden ratio', or the 'divine proportion'. Next time you see an interview on the news, look where the person is standing in the shot.

Simply put, they are probably filling one or two thirds of the screen, people rarely put their subjects in the middle of the screen anymore. Why? Because it looks better, it's more appealing and natural for us especially now we have widescreen. So when you are arranging your slides think in thirds. Fill one or two thirds of the screen, don't always centre everything. Try it and start to notice it. You'll begin to see it everywhere, in photos, paintings, food packaging, even nature. There are all sorts of calculations and ratios involved but basically think in thirds and your slides will become much more appealing to your audience.

E.g. this simple slide (that I use to explain anxiety related to presentations), has the woman's head covering around 2/3rds of the slide, this makes it look natural and appealing.

Reality!
Perceived

SEE HOW THIS FAMOUS SLIDE FROM JESSEDEE USES THIRDS. THE GUY IN THE CHAIR IS STRONGLY ON THE RIGHT HAND SIDE OF THE SCREEN, AND THE BOLD TEXT IS TO THE LEFT. THIS MAKES IT EASY ON THE EYE.

http://www.slideshare.net/jessedee/you-suck-at-powerpoint-2

DON'T DO THE DEFAULT

WHEN YOU OPEN UP POWERPOINT OR KEYNOTE YOU USUALLY GET A DEFAULT TEMPLATE OPTION. WHEN YOU SEE THAT OPTION **STOP** RIGHT THERE, GO NO FURTHER!

Do not take the default option, which is usually a main title followed by bullet-points. Instead, open a blank slide in the colour of your choice, (see elsewhere in the book for more colour advice) add a picture if you are using them, and then **if** necessary a **large** text box.

You can often change the default option too in your software's preferences or options.

Change it so you don't fall into the default trap next time you are starting up PowerPoint.

It takes a lot of discipline to do this, but so do most things worth doing.

Get a blank white template here for free – **http://leejackson.org/powerpoint-surgery-stuff**

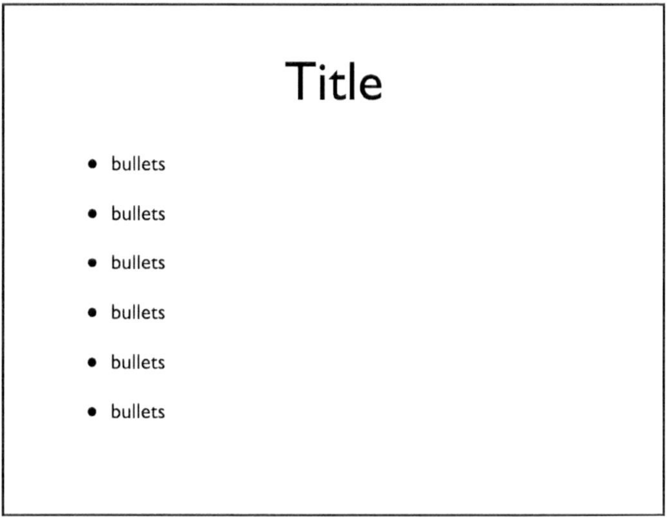

THE DEFAULT OPTION THAT TRIPS PEOPLE UP

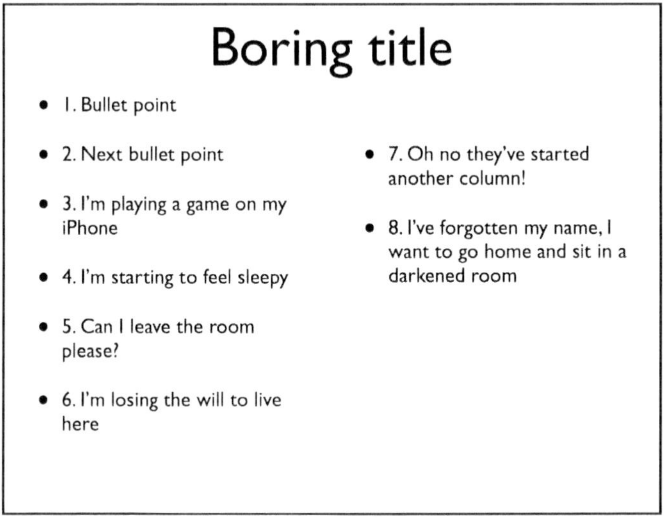
Boring title
• 1. Bullet point
• 2. Next bullet point
• 3. I'm playing a game on my iPhone
• 4. I'm starting to feel sleepy
• 5. Can I leave the room please?
• 6. I'm losing the will to live here
• 7. Oh no they've started another column!
• 8. I've forgotten my name, I want to go home and sit in a darkened room

Even simple speech bubbles make better bullets, but they are still not great
Point 1
Point 2
Point 3
Point 4
Point 5

BULLETS KILL

BULLETS DON'T JUST KILL PEOPLE, THEY KILL PRESENTATIONS TOO.

The default template may try to force you to use bullets, but you're a grown up now and as I mentioned – you can say no. Sometimes when I see speakers present a slide with bullet points you can almost feel the people in the room deflate, they may not groan out loud, but they are inside.

Sometimes people have an hour to speak using 30 slides with 10 bullet points on each slide, written in Comic Sans at font size 10. Not only do people get bored when they see this, they can read it too. People can read much faster than you can speak. Therefore if you read your bullet points, they've read ahead of you already and you are speaking 'old information' even before a word leaves your mouth. As discussed previously, people can read or listen; they can't usually do both, even if they say they can. That's why slides should be bullet-free zones, no-one likes them, they are not effective, and to be honest they are just plain lazy, we can do better than that. So for our audience's sake – please please please don't use bullets.

On a train journey I was sitting next to someone doing a research paper and she was copying her bullet points from her slides directly into her word document. They fitted perfectly, because they belonged in the word document not on the presentation slide.

I've heard it said to limit the words on a slide to 33. I'd say between 3 and 12! Any more than that then either rephrase, condense or add another slide. There are creative alternatives to bullet points, but be careful you don't just design nicer ways to bore your audience. Be tough on bullet boredom and the causes of bullet boredom.

A friend of mine who works at a well-known corporate IT company sent me their powerpoint training manual, it suggested that bullet points are fine but you shouldn't use a hierarchy of more than four deep! Ouch.

A well known I.T. company...

- ...train their staff that up to four levels of bullets are ok - this is level one
  - This is level two
    - This is level three
      - This is level four

imagine 30 slides like this!

Top Tips

- Remember this is a management reference document not a training document. It is aimed at existing not new managers
- The How To...? is designed to provide managers with one best way of delivering the Policy section
- Be clear when referencing existing briefs and documentation and state where exactly a manager can find it
- Keep information clear; concise and easy to follow
- All relevant materials must be referenced
- The manual will be on and references hyperlinked
- Keep to key actions
- is a key stakeholder to ensure all processes have hours allocated.
- Cards. These will be updated
- Be clear on timescales for activity (i.e. If it must be done on a Monday am say so)
- Flag any known issues with possible for escalation

THE ABOVE IS A REAL CORPORATE SLIDE SOMEONE SENT ME, IT HAS 11 BULLET POINTS AND OVER 100 WORDS.

“Common sense is the knack of seeing things as they are and doing things as they ought to be done.”

JOSH BILLINGS

CRUNCHING NUMBERS

COMPLEX AND INTENSE GRAPHS, DIAGRAMS AND DATA TABLES OFTEN DON'T INTEREST ANYONE WHEN YOU ARE PRESENTING BECAUSE NO-ONE CAN SEE DATA THAT'S POORLY PRESENTED.

Your audience may want to analyse the full data afterwards and that's fine – you can of course give them a hand-out in person (only ever give a hand-out after you've spoken) or online using one of the dozens of cloud options available like Dropbox, iCloud, Skydrive, Google Drive etc.

But as JesseDee[7] on Slideshare points out it's up to us to crunch the numbers for them *before* the presentation. Clear communication is our goal, so pull out the key bits of data and present them clearly, the rest is just background noise. Background noise doesn't help your message stick, clarity does. Be disciplined here and your data (if you use it) will shine to back up your message not descend on the room like a bank of fog clouding your audience's ability to see the point you're making.

JARED FANNING (JAREDFANNING.COM) TOOK THE DATA FROM SQUIDOO.COM/MOSTREADBOOKS AND BRILLIANTLY CREATED THIS INFO-GRAPHIC. DATA DOESN'T HAVE TO BE DULL. IF YOUR DATA IS KEY THEN WHY NOT GET SOMEONE TO MAKE IT LOOK GOOD?

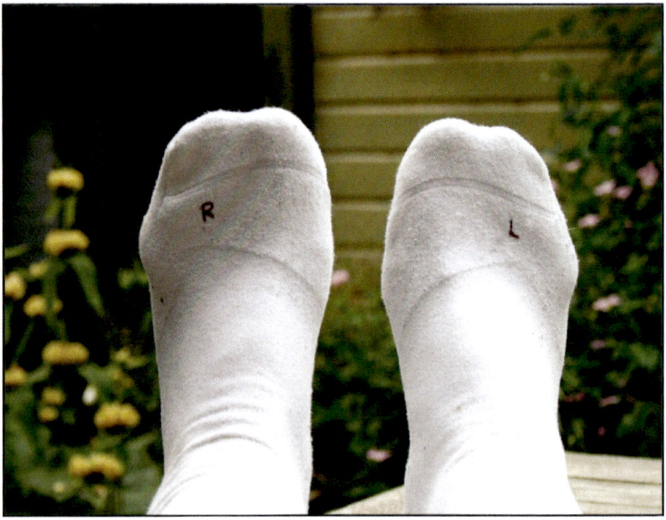
R
L

Right, Left

Right brain, left brain dominance theory[8] is often quoted and exaggerated. It's true that the right side of our brain is best at expressive, musical and creative tasks. It's also true that the left side of our brain is better at logical, analytical and language tasks. In our presentations and slide design we should bear this in mind, but we must also not overdo it. Our brains just don't divide that way in real life and recent research shows that to learn certain skills well we use both sides of our brain. So, design for both sides and you'll hit everyone. It's wrong to think that a presentation to accountants needs to be all logic and nothing creative. There are many 'creative' accountants out there, and I mean that in the most positive way, not the off-shore tax haven kind of way!

FONTS GET CAR SICK

LET ME BE BLUNT, (AS IF I HAVEN'T BEEN ALREADY) SOME FONTS ARE GREAT, SOME SUCK, AND SOME JUST SCREAM LAZINESS.

The laziest of all fonts is, of course, Times New Roman, mainly because it's the first one on offer (as Don McMillan points out on his comedy Youtube video[9]). It's more at home in long, public sector "death by PowerPoint" health and safety briefings. Coming in a close second is Comic Sans! Comic Sans has been the go-to font for primary school teachers and church notice sheets for years, it needs to be banned, in fact it's so bad that there is a movement to do just that – http://bancomicsans.com. It was designed for use in comic speech bubbles, and nowhere else, so if you're not designing a comic, please don't use it. Ok I'll take a deep breath, and go to my happy place...right, I'm back in the room. Using eye-catching fonts is a great way to make your slides stickier, but there are a couple of downsides to discovering free font websites. Firstly is that we can go a bit mad, from a 15 year diet of Times New Roman we can suddenly flip and use Back to the future, Top Gun and Star Wars fonts everywhere. Beware of the dark side. A good rule of thumb is to use one or two clear fonts **only** in a whole presentation and even then maybe take them from a similar 'font family' (sans serif fonts are often best for clarity). The second problem that I've had to learn the hard way is that I've made a great presentation with a couple of killer fonts, I've saved it to a USB stick, plugged it into another laptop to do my presentation, and all of a sudden my killer font has been magically transformed into Times New Roman! Arrghhh! It even happens on the iPad too – you may have experienced this. Basically fonts don't travel well, they get car sick and often don't make the journey at all. So beware, the only solutions to this problem are...

1 Save the presentation with "embedded fonts" (although this only works properly in some versions of presentation software and it's still a risk in my opinion)

2 Take all the fonts as files onto the USB stick you use with you to install on the laptop (can be risky especially if you don't have admin rights on the laptop at the venue as often happens)

3 Save your presentation as jpegs (pictures) or as a PDF and import the presentation back into your programme slide by slide, save it again and take that one. (This is time consuming and un-editable, but it works)

4 My preferred option is to take my own laptop with me and only use that. I put this into my 'rider' for events (along with two packs of organic prawn cocktail crisps, a big bowl of blue M&M's and fresh spring water direct from the Yorkshire Dales*). By doing this, what you see is what you get, and a nice side effect of this is that you feel more comfortable using your own laptop and therefore are less nervous as a result. It means carrying your laptop but you probably do that anyway. Enjoy new fonts, but exercise control and restraint and you'll be fine.

**not strictly true.*

In 2012 the British comedian Dave Gorman sold out and then extended his nation-wide tour. It was called 'Dave Gorman's PowerPoint Presentation'. People like good shows even if they do include PowerPoint slides!

Don't do a talk, put on a show.

Opposite are some slides from my main motivational presentation (How to enjoy and succeed at work/education). The whole two hours and the main points (based on solid research) are in this case displayed as high contrast fonts on a black background. The last one is simply a card that I give out to people to make the points memorable, after the event – the fonts make it stand out. If it was in Times New Roman it would be instantly forgettable.

PASSION
work
hard
PUSH
THRU
IDEAS
GET
GOOD
FOCUS
(ON THE RIGHT THING
AT THE RIGHT TIME)
KEEP ON
GOING!
serve
RRR
PASSION
work hard
FOCUS
PUSH
THRU
IDEAS
GET
GOOD
serve
KEEP ON
RRR
GOING!
What was your "DING!" moment? twitter: @leejackson

IMAGES: THIS ISN'T THE 90'S

HOME ALONE, WAYNE'S WORLD AND TITANIC WERE KING IN THE 90'S – ALONG WITH CLIPART.

People couldn't get enough of quirky hand drawn stick figures with question marks above their heads. Then as the 90's progressed we moved into cheesy stock photos, and we were all introduced to that picture of the world with two anonymous business people's hands shaking in front of it. I still see that now.

Some people even used sounds on their slides, a "bing" to announce the change of slide, a "clunk" to wake up the audience when a new bullet point appears. We loved it. Those days have gone. We might like watching Titanic again once in a while (the boat sinks by the way, a friend of ours didn't realise that and she was gutted when it happened in the film) but we really need to drag our slides into this decade.

Here's how: ditch the clipart, sounds and cheesy stock pictures and go for big pictures that **fill** the screen.

Choose your pictures carefully, never choose the most popular photos on stock sites (see the techie section near the end of this book for more help) and make sure the image is big enough to fill the screen without getting grainy or pixelated. That makes a big difference. Remember your laptop screen is fairly small and a big screen will show up all the imperfections in the image, so buy or find decent size images but not too big so they get too unwieldy.

Use 'random internet' or 'Googled' images with caution, beware of copyright and quality. Most of us have phones with good cameras on these days so why not use your own photos and start building up your own library of images? Flickr creative commons is also a good option for images you can use with permission, see **http://www.flickr.com/creativecommons**. Stock image websites are big business and come in all shapes and sizes. I use Big Stock Photo as they are user-friendly and great value compared to many out there. You can use the link below to get 20% off one of their image packs: **http://www.bigstockphoto.com/promo/PRE51Ns**

3 great tips from the team at Haikudeck.com for choosing images

1 **Don't limit yourself to literal:** There's no need to get stuck on a specific search word or phrase, try zooming out and exploring different angles in to your topic. For example, if you're making a "Summer Road Trip" slide deck, try evocative phrases like "highway" or "scenic route" if "summer vacation" or "road trip" isn't doing the trick.

2 **Go abstract:** Some text is just tough to illustrate visually. Abstract images are a great way to add some aesthetic mojo to your slide without distracting your audience from its message. Try searching for "light" and "pattern," for example.

3 **Explore emotional triggers:** Sometimes you're trying to illustrate a feeling like fear, joy, or unbearable itchiness. Instead of searching for the emotions themselves, try searching for what would invoke that feeling, whether it's extreme heights, tasty pastries, or wool sweaters.

If you hit a dead end with your image searching, try a different tack and keep exploring! When we're creative with our keywords, and willing to go beyond the first few image results, we often get inspired by a new, unexpected creative direction.

CASE STUDY

GEOFF RAMM

Another tip that many great speakers employ is to use images from the place where you are speaking. So, if you're speaking away from home, don't use images of your home town, use people and places your audience would know, they love it!

Here, international marketing speaker Geoff Ramm (**@geofframm**) uses a local cryptic slide for his audience in Iran. The clue then reveals a local florist business that he went into on Kish Island in Iran. The slide then launches him into a story of local marketing, he won the speaker of the conference award, three times. He now owns three Persian rugs!

BLOOMIN
KISH
Advertising
چهارمین مجمع جهانی
تبلیغات

Learn to 'bleed' your images...

Learn to 'bleed' your images

Learn to bleed...

...in other words drag the image off the edges of the screen so there are no gaps around the image or slide. Play about with it and you can get all sorts of effects i.e. instead of using a full person's face, drag the image off the screen and use two thirds. It can make your slides striking. Many image effects are reliant on having a big enough image to start with. Get creative with large images that fill the screen, not cutesy 90's clipart scattered randomly.

1 2 3 4 5 6 7 8 9 10
1: Where is this issue on a scale of 1 - 10?

1 2 3 4 5 6 7 8 9 10
1: Where is this issue on a scale of 1 - 10?

CASE STUDY

PAUL MCGEE

I worked with bestselling author / speaker Paul McGee (**@thesumoguy**). He uses great cartoons in his work, but by simply suggesting we enlarged the cartoon, changed the background colour and dropped the small logo I think it makes for a much more striking and memorable set of slides. Simple tweaks can make a big difference.

“

Communication is the transfer of emotion...logic is not enough...create slides that reinforce your words not repeat them.[10]

SETH GODIN

”

BY READING OUT YOUR SLIDES OR BULLET POINTS YOU ARE EITHER MAKING YOUR SLIDES OR YOURSELF REDUNDANT. DON'T MAKE YOURSELF REDUNDANT.

Use 'text holders' to highlight your text

Once you have large pictures filling the screen you may want to add one or more words of text. One way to do that well is to use a text holder, as often text can get lost when put directly onto images. Using a text holder eradicates that i.e. make the text holder black and your text white or vice-versa and it will stand out wherever you put it on the slide. Be creative, you could also use images to place text onto like a piece of masking tape, a torn piece of paper, a post-it note from stock photo sites etc...

...with a text placeholder!

...with a text placeholder!

CASE STUDY

CLAIRE YOUNG

BBC The Apprentice finalist and speaker Claire Young (**@claireLyoung**) originally had three bits of info on one slide, I suggested making it into three slides

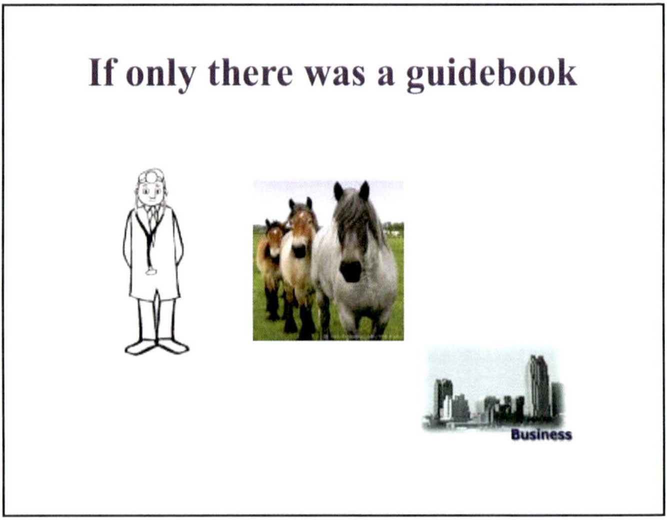

If only there was a guidebook!
If only there was a guidebook!
Ideas
Brainstorming
Business Plan
Clients
Market Analysis
Testing
Marketing
Finished Product
Delivery
If only there was a guidebook!

> **"Although I began by making fun of (PowerPoint), I soon realised I could actually create things that were beautiful."**
>
> **DAVID BYRNE**[11]

SPACE IS YOUR FRIEND

AS GOOD DESIGNERS WILL SAY – TO AMPLIFY, SIMPLIFY.

The average slide has around 30-40 words on it. When you use text on a slide can you limit it to 3-12 words as previously mentioned? Give it a go, if you still think you need more words then simply start another slide. Our temptation is always to fill the space we've got on a slide. We add logos, email addresses, website addresses, phone numbers and all sorts of other things because we think we need to. This does two things. One, it makes our slides all look the same, and two, it limits the space we have to play with. If you need to, put all your details on 'bumper' slides. Put a picture and all your contact details tastefully on one slide and show it at the beginning as you are introduced and then again at the end of your session as you grab your stuff to leave, or do a Q+A. Branding experts have done much to help us get rid of bad logos and colour schemes but they have also inadvertently killed many PowerPoint slides by making us feel that we have to have our branding on every slide. Branding is useful, and keeping certain colours and fonts is ideal to keep subtle branding throughout a presentation, but don't feel forced to add extra stuff to your slides. Designers know that blank space works well – that's why they don't fill it. If you've ever been in an Apple store you'll know what I mean. There's hardly anything there! They use space well and it draws us in. Next time you are in a shopping centre pop into Primark or your local pound shop. Compare and contrast with an Apple store or Bang and Olufsen. Good design is restrained so our slides should be too…

You can't use big images if theres no room for them. Let the images speak not boring templates.

© Lee Jackson
Presentation title
Event title
www.leejackson.biz
My logo
Todays date
lee@leejackson.org
www.leejackson.biz

If the screen is moving
in the background they
won't look at you (and
that is a bad thing!)

...MOTION DISTRACTS

NINJAS WEAR BLACK AND ARE TRAINED TO MOVE SLOWLY AND SMOOTHLY BECAUSE MOTION ATTRACTS ATTENTION.

(I saw this in a film once. I haven't trained as a ninja but like most blokes I claim to be an expert in all forms of useless knowledge including martial arts training!). If you are speaking, the slide behind you should be stationary and not moving, flashing, whizzing, whirring or zooming in and out. People's focus needs to be on you not your screen – if something is happening behind you they won't concentrate on you and your message. Slides should be a backdrop that add to your talk and not a fruit machine that's trying to attract your attention. When people hear that I'm a slide expert they sometimes talk about their slides (like comedians have jokes told to them), and often they show me a new animation or slide transition that they've found.[12] I smile politely because I am nice, however I use very few transitions now at all because they simply slow me down and just aren't needed. Use your voice and body language to move people onto a new place in your presentation, not a new fancy slide transition. I've seen training days and webinars devoted to slide animations *alone*, I really don't see the point, they usually add nothing to the stickiness of our message. The only exception to this rule is speaker Richard McCann who tells his life story using photos of him as a child, the photos fade to black after a few seconds bringing the attention back to him as a speaker. The very subtle fade effect he uses even seems to add depth to his story somehow.

USING VIDEO

I USE VIDEO CLIPS QUITE A LOT, BUT IT'S TAKEN ME YEARS TO GET IT RIGHT.

Be very careful using video as there are so many things that can go wrong – the obvious copyright issues, loss of sound, not playing at all, 'lag' (sound and vision being out of sync) etc. My advice is simple – if you have a new-ish Mac running Apple Keynote, you're onto a winner, as in my experience, it handles video so much better than a PC running PowerPoint. This is also another reason to always use your own laptop for your presentation.

As with static slides though, the same advice stands: does it add anything? If so then make your video full screen then check it works well again and again **before** your presentation.

I always think of videos as launching pads (not landing mats), in other words, they should highlight and take your presentation to a new place, and they should say something new in a creative way.

(You may also find that downloading and installing a 'codec pack' may also help with playback. See my techie tips later in this book for more information.)

Your slides may be killing your business. If a member of your team was letting you down constantly, you'd do something about it. When slides are letting us down, it's strange that we often continue to do what we've always done.

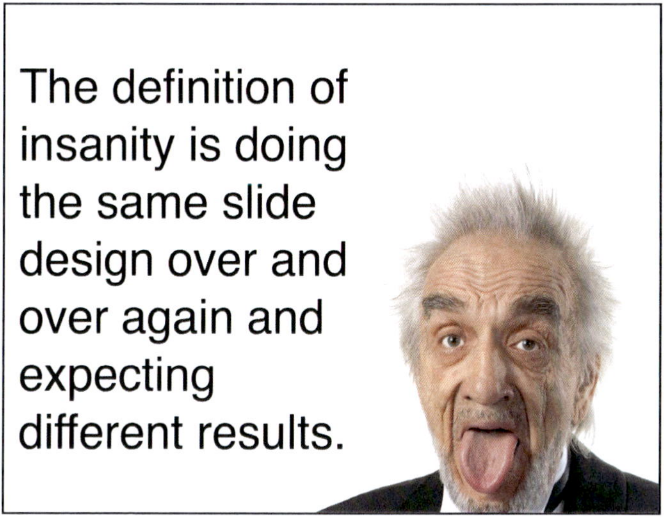

(NOT ALBERT EINSTEIN'S QUOTATION, JUST LIKE THE ORIGINAL QUOTE ISN'T EITHER!)

"People are asking whether, ultimately PowerPoint makes us all stupid, or does it help us streamline our thoughts?[13]"

PETER NORVIG
GOOGLE ENGINEERING DIRECTOR

ASK FOR FEEDBACK

IF YOU ARE PREPARING A PRESENTATION, HOPEFULLY YOU'LL TRY IT OUT ON SOMEONE WHOSE OPINION YOU VALUE AND ASK THEM FOR SOME FEEDBACK.

Don't forget to do that with your slides too, but please don't ask someone who uses bad slides. Go outside of your workplace, get out of your office and ask someone who will really tell you the truth. Get your presentation slides onto a big monitor or screen and view them from the back of the room, view them sitting down. Can you see them clearly? What do the edges of the slides look like? Are the slides transitioning ok? Check, check and check again and then be brave enough to ask a couple of people for their feedback. You'll be glad you did.

Apparently feedback is the breakfast of champions, I personally prefer porridge.

CASE STUDY

DR. EMMA SUTTON

(**@nakedpresenting**)

Here, Emma introduces us to a simple set of slides featuring her hand-drawn character Lucy, the story of her presentation is simple and the slides back that up. Keeping them clean and simple really brings power to her talk. People remember Lucy too, and because they remember Lucy they remember the message.

Mine for
Your
Diamond
Dr Emma Sutton
@nakedpresenting

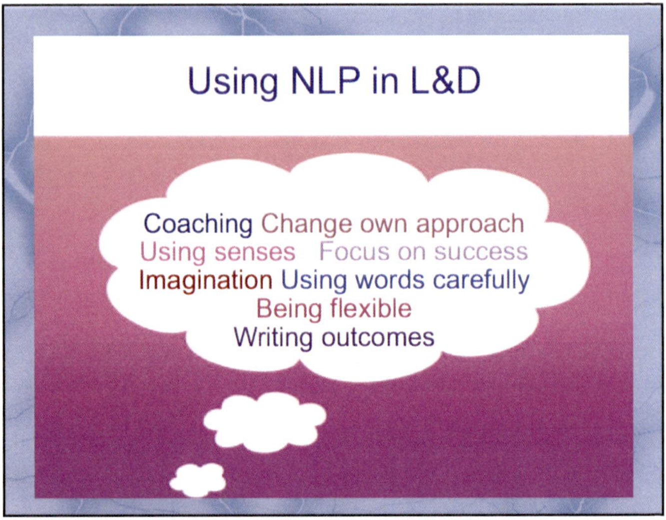
Using NLP in L&D
Coaching Change own approach
Using senses Focus on success
Imagination Using words carefully
Being flexible
Writing outcomes

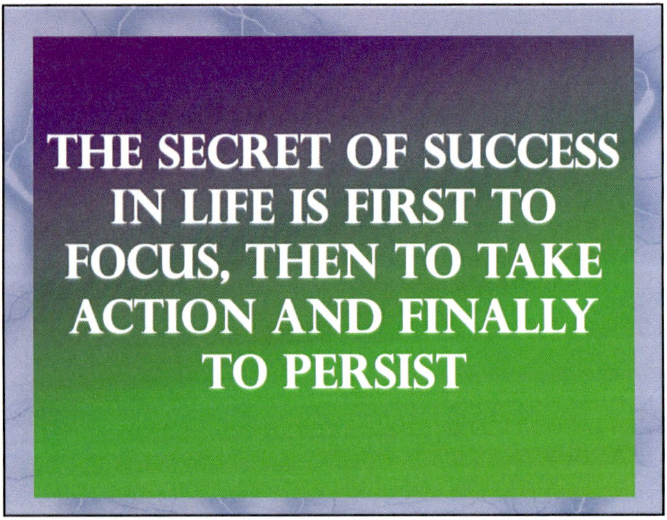
THE SECRET OF SUCCESS IN LIFE IS FIRST TO FOCUS, THEN TO TAKE ACTION AND FINALLY TO PERSIST

...THE BAD AND THE UGLY...

I'd love to show you a lot of the bad examples out there online too but I don't want to get sued, so just Google "Bad powerpoint" and enjoy the ride!

But, here's a few that people have sent me – I've re-written/designed them hiding identities but they are as they were sent, warts and all. No exaggerations.

What do you think is wrong with them? Would you have been keen to sit through an hour of someone reading these?

My friend sent me some of her old slides as a confession (opposite), she has since seen the error of her ways, but was kind enough to share!

(logo removed)

What is a disqualification order and what is its purpose?

- *"The primary purpose of* [s.6 disqualification] *is not to punish the individual but to protect the public against the future conduct of companies by persons whose past records as directors of insolvent companies have shown them to be a danger to creditors and others"*

(Browne-Wilkinson V.C. in *Re Lo-Line Electric Motors Ltd [1988] Ch. 477 at 486*)

- **Company Directors Disqualification Act 1986 ("the CDDA")**
- **s.1(1)** In the circumstances specified below in this Act a court may, and under sections 6 and 9A shall, make against a person a disqualification order, that is to say an order that for a period specified in the order -
  - (a) he shall not be a director of a company, act as receiver of a company's property or in any way, whether directly or indirectly, be concerned or take part in the promotion, formation or management of a company unless (in each case) he has the leave of the court, and
  - (b) he shall not act as an insolvency practitioner.

THESE ARE REAL SLIDES FROM LAWYERS (ALL I'VE DONE IS REMOVE A LOGO FROM THE TOP RIGHT HAND CORNER), THE BOTTOM ONE IS THE 72ND SLIDE IN THE DECK!

Disqualification undertakings

- **s.1A(1)** In the circumstances specified in sections 7 and 8 the Secretary of State may accept a disqualification undertaking, that is to say an undertaking by any person that, for a period specified in the undertaking, the person -
  - (a) will not be a director of a company, act as a receiver of a company's property or in any way, whether directly or indirectly, be concerned or take part in the promotion, formation or management of a company unless (in each case) he has the leave of the court, and
  - (b) will not act as an insolvency practitioner.

- **s.7(2A)** If it appears to the Secretary of State that the conditions mentioned in section 6(1) are satisfied as respects any person who has offered to five him a disqualification undertaking, he may accept the undertaking if it appears to him that it is expedient in the public interest that he should do so (instead of applying, or proceedings with an application, for a disqualification order).

When is an order made?

- **s.6(1)** The court shall make a disqualification order against a person in any case here, on an application under this section, it is satisfied -
  - (a) that he is or has been a director of a company which has at any time become insolvent (whether while he was a director or subsequently), and
  - (b) that his conduct as a director of that company (either taken alone or taken together with his conduct as a director of any other company or companies) makes him unfit to be concerned in the management of a company.

- **s.7(1)** If it appears to the Secretary of State that it is <u>expedient in the public interest</u> that a disqualification order under section 6 should be made against any person, an application for the making of such an order against that person may be made -
  - (a) by the Secretary of State, or
  - (b) if the Secretary of State so directs in the case of a person who is or has been a director of a company which is being wound up by the court in England and Wales, by the official receiver.

When is an order made?

- **s.2** Disqualification on conviction of an indictable offence
- **s.3** Disqualification for persistent breaches of companies legislation
- **s.4** Disqualification for fraud, etc., in winding up
- **s.5** Disqualification on summary conviction
- **s.8** Disqualification after investigation of company
- **s.9A** Competition disqualification order
- **s.10** Participation in wrongful trading
- **s.12** Failure to pay under county court administration order

- **s.11** Undischarged bankrupts

(this was slide 72!)

THE 3 DINGS

THERE ARE 3 THINGS THAT HAVE BEEN 'DING MOMENTS' WHEN I'VE BEEN SPEAKING UP FRONT.

The first was when totally by accident I told an unplanned off-the-cuff personal story to a very bored group of teens when I was a youth worker many years ago. As I was speaking I suddenly realised that I had their full attention, I was shocked. **The power of story should never be underestimated** as the best way to connect to an audience and for an audience to remember and act on your message. I remember talks from years ago because I remember a certain story a speaker told. Only the other day my friend David Taylor recounted a story that a speaker he saw used over a decade ago, the image of the cow used in the story on the slide he used helped him recount the whole talk after all these years.

The second was when I realised that to be a great speaker I had to be me – Lee Jackson. I know this sounds pretty obvious, but when that penny dropped it changed my life. Don't ever try to be something or someone else. When I coach people in their presentations this comes up time and again. We have to be ourselves when giving a presentation, or more accurately we have to be ourselves plus 25% for greatest impact.

The third 'ding moment' is why I wrote this book. When people were giving me feedback I saw that they had noticed my visuals. I hope you get great feedback on your presentations and visuals too. If you use them, the two elements come as a package, so work hard on them both for maximum impact.

I interviewed slide guru Nancy Duarte (the author of Slide:ology, Resonate and the person behind Al Gore's famous slides in the film 'An Inconvenient Truth'.) I asked her to distil her presentation philosophy into one phrase.

She said:

"OUR GOLDEN RULE IS, NEVER DELIVER A PRESENTATION THAT YOU WOULDN'T WANT TO SIT THROUGH YOURSELF."

I like that.

"We've noticed"
"We've noticed"
"I know this isn't very good"

CONFESSION TIME

WITH ALL THIS SAID, I DO HAVE A CONFESSION TO MAKE. I'VE DONE IT ALL WRONG IN THE PAST.

I've used bad colour schemes, clip art, poor fonts and I've probably used slides when I didn't need to. Even now one of my motivational keynote talks has 37 slides. BUT, before you throw things at me, they are *all* big, bold and they do add to my presentation. I only have one slide of bullet points (which is a quiz used only in longer presentations) and there are no off-putting transitions. Oh yeah, and I only look at the screen once in an hour, and that's when I'm making a point with a line graph like Peter Snow on election night and I do that mainly for a change of pace and focus. The rest of the time I'm interacting directly with my audience.

Reading verbatim from slides is not a no-no, it's **THE** no-no.

This isn't a pure presentation skills book as such, that'll come later, but I must say this...when we are speaking, people come first, their time is very precious, so our goal should always be clarity of message and engagement with the audience, not just 'nicer slides'.

IN A NUTSHELL

ASK 'DO I NEED SLIDES?'

If so...accept responsibility for your slides. Understand you ARE a designer. Think billboard not document. They are not your script. Don't do the default. Bullets kill presentations. Crunch the numbers beforehand and only show the key figures. Enjoy new fonts but remember they don't travel well. Ditch the cheesy clip art and pics. Use full screen photos and text holders. Cut out the motion. Ask for honest feedback.

To amplify, **simplify**.

Or, to make it even briefer, when designing your slides, keep them **simple**.

Do slides right and your presentation will be enhanced, and never forget **the power of story**.

Prepare well, speak about what you know, be passionate, keep your slides simple and enjoy the experience.

great
slides
in a
nutshell

> **In my opinion Powerpoint slides with long lists of what you're talking about should be banned. They are used as a prop by the speaker – if they need reminding of what they're speaking about they can have it on a laptop in front of them. There are few things worse than watching someone talk through a long list of Powerpoints. On the other hand short videos and photos bring a talk to life.**
>
> **RICHARD BRANSON**[14]

A few techie tips to make your presentation even better...

Use a grid

When displaying more than one thing like logos for example, don't use the tag lines and extra stuff just keep them basic and align them on an invisible line or grid, which will make them much more pleasing to the eye and professional. Grids help for all sorts of things and the automatic grid on Apple iWork Keynote is one of the reasons I love the software so much. If your software doesn't have a grid, just make one or download one free from my website – **http://leejackson.org/powerpoint-surgery-stuff**

Choose a 'clicker' well

A clicker prevents you having to be tied to your laptop and is well worth the investment. There's nothing worse than a presenter walking back to their laptop every two minutes to change to the next slide. I'd suggest using a good brand name like Keyspan or Logitech not an anonymous generic one and try it out a lot before you use it live. I use one with a volume control and a pause button which is very useful for video work on iWork Keynote.

Colour

To choose good colours, Google a colour theme picker like **http://kuler.adobe.com** and then use the eyedropper tool in your slide software to match your colours well. Also check that you remove the background colours too so things don't look 'plonked there' and don't ever use a gradient, they look naff and very 1990's. If you need to change or remove a background colour you can use 'instant alpha' on Apple iWork Keynote or use photo manipulation software. If you're not a techie type then you can always beg a friend or colleague to help or use a website like **fiverr.com** where someone can do it for a fiver ($5).

Fonts

There are loads of free font websites out there, I like **http://dafont.com** as it's very easy to navigate. Fonts are usually installed by just double clicking on them. Give it a go. You can even get your own handwriting made into a font for that personal touch **http://www.yourfonts.com/fontgenerator/342330.html**

Video codecs

If you are using video, you are entering the complex world of copyright, video formats and 'codecs'. There are many different formats to use video you'll see .mov .mpeg .avi .wmv amongst many others at the end of the file name. The easiest way to make sure that your laptop will play these formats is to install a 'codec pack'. I cannot advise you directly as these change all the time, so simply Google 'best codec pack for PC/mac', read the reviews and take your pick. In the past I've used different ones but depending on when you are reading this, they may have been superseded as the internet moves pretty fast. That's why you should always Google hard and read up before installation. But, take heed, there have been times when I've spent ages trying to edit or to get a video to work and in the end I didn't really need it. Always ask "Do I really need this?" as it could save you hours of work.

There's an app for that

Have you seen any of the presentation apps for iPads and tablets yet? Look up Slideshark, Keynote and Haiku Deck for starters. The future looks bright for mobile presenting, but the same rules apply: if these apps don't help you, your message or your audience, beware. I love gadgets and apps but it's easy to get carried away. Clarity is key; not the latest technology.

Go deeper...

http://en.wikipedia.org/wiki/Golden_ratio

Books:

Presentation Zen: Simple Ideas on Presentation Design and Delivery by Garr Reynolds

Slide:ology: The Art and Science of Creating Great Presentations by Nancy Duarte

Resonate: Present Visual Stories That Transform Audiences by Nancy Duarte

Rethinking PowerPoint: Improving Presentations With Techniques That Engage The Mind by Allyssa Ritch and Ron Galloway

Made to Stick by Chip and Dan Heath

Slideshare.net also has the good the bad and the very ugly, this one I think is probably the best there is: **http://www.slideshare.net/jessedee/you-suck-at-PowerPoint-2**

Some good stuff here too: **http://www.slideshare.net/dednie**

Discovering the Power of PowerPoint: Rethinking the Design of Presentation Slides from a Skilful User's Perspective Michael Alley / Kathryn A. Neeley Virginia Tech /University of Virginia: **http://www.tcc.virginia.edu/LEE2008/ASEE%202005%20Final %20Version.pdf**

Stop press!

At the time of writing I've just spent three days helping a big corporate client to communicate better including spending a lot of time helping them to simplify their slide design. After my trip abroad I was on the train home and the guy sitting opposite me was working on his slides for a presentation at a conference. As I peeked round to see them (I couldn't help myself!) I could tell they were possibly the worst slides I'd ever seen, with the smallest font I'd ever seen, there was dozens of them too!

Battles are being won in this area, but the war against bad slides continues.

Thank you for playing your part!

BIGSTOCK

Don't forget you can use the link below to get 20% off BigStockPhoto.com stock image credit packs…

http://www.bigstockphoto.com/promo/PRE51Ns

Enjoy!

(Unless stated all images in this book are from the author, contributors or from www.bigstockphoto.com and are used with their kind permission.)

Snow
NOW IS THE
WINTER OF OUR
DISCO TENT

Footnotes

1 It's possible I may have 'remixed' their content as I've read and listened to their stuff for years now. I have tried my best to source everything, but please do tell me about any omissions so I can put that right in future editions. Advice on slides is always finite and so no plagiarism was ever intentional of course.

2 http://www.robertgaskins.com/

3 http://www.wired.com/wired/archive/11.09/ppt2.html

4 My friend is an audio-visual guy and does lots of corporate events, he contacted me recently and said an organiser had just told him to turn down the lights as the slides are more important than the presenter, he did as he was told, and, yes, the event was terrible.

5 Principles of Educational Multimedia User Interface Design, Dr. LAWRENCE J. NAJJAR, Georgia Tech Research Institute, Atlanta, Georgia

6 http://en.wikipedia.org/wiki/Cognitive_load#Cognitive_load_theory

7 http://www.slideshare.net/jessedee

8 http://psychology.about.com/od/cognitivepsychology/a/left-brain-right-brain.htm

9 Don McMillan's youtube video:
http://www.youtube.com/watch?v=MjcO2ExtHso

10 http://sethgodin.typepad.com/seths_blog/2007/01/really_bad_powe.html

11 http://www.wired.com/wired/archive/11.09/ppt1.html

12 The same applies for Prezi – people keep asking me if I use Prezi, at the moment I don't because I've never seen anyone use it without making me feel seasick. Too much motion for me at the moment, but of course it's only a tool, and at this stage of it's development I've only seen it used clunkily, to be honest. I'm sure there are great examples out there but I just haven't seen them in person yet.

13 http://www.edwardtufte.com/bboard/q-and-a-fetch-msg?msg_id=0000iF&topic_id=1

14 http://www.linkedin.com/today/post/article/20130215121303-204068115-top-5-tips-to-screw-businessmeetings-as-usual